the museum
of impressionism
in Paris

the museum of impressionism in Paris

INTRODUCTION BY THÉRÈSE BUROLLET
BRIEF NOTES
ON THE PAINTERS
BY FRANÇOIS MATHEY

fernand hazan éditeur

35-37, RUE DE SEINE, PARIS VI

THE NOTES ON FANTIN-LATOUR AND ROUSSEAU
ARE WRITTEN BY PIERRE GEORGEL.

THE GALLERIES OF THE JEU DE PAUME and the Orangerie were placed under the care of the Director of the Musée du Luxembourg in 1927, for the exhibition of foreign painting and Impressionist pictures belonging to the state. These had been piled up for a long time in a small room that made viewing from a suitable distance impossible. After a brief period in the Louvre, they were at last found a large gallery and satisfactory hanging space in the Jeu de Paume. It was built in the reign of Napoléon III, altered in 1877, then in 1932 and completely renovated in 1959. The Galerie du Jeu de Paume, usually called the Musée de l'Impressionnisme, contains most of the Impressionist works owned by the state and particularly the donations made by Caillebotte (1894/96), Moreau-Nélaton (1906), Isaac de Camondo (1911) and Gachet (1951/54). They are not, however, all gathered together there, for the important Personnaz Collection (1937) is still exhibited in the Louvre to illustrate the final development of 19th century painting in the rooms devoted to it. Although the Musée du Jeu de Paume does not house all the Impressionist paintings it possesses, on the other hand, the works of several painters who were only on the fringes of Impressionism, like Degas, Cézanne, Van Gogh; who transformed it like Seurat and Signac; or who had completely freed themselves from its influence, like Gauguin and Odilon Redon. The Museum of Late 19th Century Painting would be a more appropriate name for this collection if it did not utterly ignore the representatives of official art. It is in this disdain of gallery directors today for so-called "academic" painting that there lies the principal connecting link between the life and work of all the artists represented here. Although they are not all Impressionists, far from it in fact, and although they have neither the same way of looking at things nor the same techniques, they were all forced by the hostility of the representatives of established art to form groups and stand shoulder to shoulder in an attempt to make a precarious living and produce their independent works. These painters never founded a school or even a group to fight for recognition of their aesthetic ideas. Quite the contrary. Although they were fiercely attached to their independence and wanted to shake off the yoke of traditional teaching, they pursued their solitary paths, their own way of interpreting a personal vision of the world. They got on well together, exchanged ideas and shared each other's experiments as so many painters had done before them, but their conversations did not take place in the studios of the École des Beaux-Arts or in the rooms of the French school at Rome. They followed the example of the Barbizon painters' evening discussions in Père Ganne's inn, or the landscapists, Boudin, Courbet and Jongkind, who gathered together at Mère Toutain's, in the farm of Saint-Siméon near Honfleur. They left for the country in little groups: Monet and Renoir to Bougival (1869), Manet, Monet, Renoir, Sisley and Caillebotte to Argenteuil (1874), Cézanne, Pissarro, Guillaumin then Van Gogh to stay with Dr Gachet at Auvers-sur-Oise. But Paris was more than anywhere else the meeting place of the Impressionists, where they would gather together nearly every evening at the Café Guerbois in the avenue de Clichy. Manet used to invite to dinner Renoir, Degas, Bazille, Guillaumin, Fantin-Latour and Desboutins and there they would meet effervescent critics like Zola, Astuc, Duret and Duranty. Courbet sometimes came to share their discussions and Monet, Pissarro, Sisley and Cézanne himself joined them when they visited the capital. These young men came to find moral support among their friends, but, more even than this, they valued the exchange of ideas, which they missed in their solitary work. They never, however, thought of drawing up a plan of action. Although these meetings ended with producing on the 15th May, 1874, a group exhibition on the premises of the photographer, Nadar, at 35 boulevard des Capucines, it was only after ten years of rebuffs from the organizers of the Salon. The revolt which the Impressionists showed on this occasion and which moreover ended with a useless scandal, was not characteristic of them. Although they rejected academic art and refused to train at the École des Beaux-Arts, it was only to escape the clutches of tradition and the shackles of conventional art. Once they had won their creative freedom, they would have liked to have exhibited their works in peace without any battles and polemics.

Apart from Manet, who was Couture's pupil, and Degas, who attended Lamothe's class, the Impressionists used to work almost on their own at the Académie Suisse or Gleyre's Atelier. Their training was particularly friendly, because they shared the same studios, the same experiments and the same anxieties. Bazille suggests vividly the atmosphere of this work pursued in common in the *Studio* (1870), a painting which lacks the fine qualities of Fantin-Latour's *Studio at Batignolles* (1870), but which gives us a homely picture of the friendly

7

relationships of the group. The Impressionists very soon turned to working in the open air on the advice of Monet and following the example of Boudin, who was already working on the motif (*Beach in Normandy*, 1865). Manet and Degas seldom went further afield than painting public gardens and race-courses (Degas, *Racehorses in front of the Grandstand*, 1869/72), but the genuine Impressionists found that the essence of their art lay in capturing variations of light and the fluidity of atmosphere. It made them want to paint light reflected off rainy streets (Pissarro, *The Stage-Coach*, 1877), the dazzle of sun on the river (Monet, *The Seine at Vétheuil*, 1879), shadows on snow (Sisley, *Snow at Louveciennes*, 1878), bright flowers in sunny fields (Monet, *The Poppies*, 1873). The people they painted were grouped outside in the hard light of summer (Monet, *Women in the Garden*, 1867), or the halflight of woods, delicately toned by the sun filtering through the leaves (Monet, *Le Déjeuner sur l'Herbe*, 1865/66). Light was always the real subject of a painting for the Impressionists. Monet, at the end of his life, went so far as to paint the same subject several times in a different light (the two series of the *Cathedral*, 1894 and the *Water-lilies*, 1904). They had a presentiment of the primary importance of color diffused by shadows and the transformation of local color by the constant interaction of tones on each other; they worked out instinctively the principle of applying broken colors by juxtaposing patches of pure tones that are recomposed on the retina at a distance into the sensation of the required color. This interpretation of the law of simultaneous contrasts was only empirical with the Impressionists. Seurat and Signac worked out its theory. Neo-impressionism was based on the scientific discoveries of Chevreul (1839) and Rood (1875) and consisted of the systematic division of touches of color (Seurat, *Back View of a Model*, 1887). This divisionist technique was not the only link of the painters with science.   Degas, for example, was very struck by the successive stages of movement and no longer tried to suggest a moment of fleeting light, but an instant of movement caught in its trajectory: a horse in full gallop (*The Gentlemen's Race,* 1862) or a poised dancer (*End of an Arabesque,* 1877).   Some writers on the Impressionists have attached great importance to the modernity, so dear to Baudelaire.   The essential aim of these painters was to convey in their work as brief a moment of life as possible, without looking for its eternal aspect.   This is why the subject meant little to artists who painted it from nature, giving the maximum effect to the impressions they received to the exclusion of all literary content or historic context.   Consequently, it cannot be asserted that they set out to paint a picture of their period, its fashions and discoveries. Admittedly, they recorded it as any painter conditioned by his times has done, but without feeling any particular concern to stress its importance.   There is hardly more modernity to be found in Monet's *Women in the Garden* than in Winterhalter's *The Empress Eugénie with the Ladies of the Court ;* in Manet's portrait of *Clemenceau* (1880) than in Bonnat's of *Thiers* (1877, Musée Bonnat, Bayonne); in Degas' *Women Ironing* (1884) than in Lhermitte's *Harvesters' Wages* (1882).   The Impressionists seized on anything in everyday life that satisfied their aesthetic and their vision of the world: happy children, fond young mothers, women strolling under their parasols, sunny gardens and noisy resorts of pleasure.   They loved, too, barges on melancholy canals, flooded countrysides and stations veiled with smoke.   They were fascinated by the city and the scintillating life of its streets; they painted the boulevards, brightly lit theatres and the sadness of its cafés.

The impossibility of conforming to the traditional notions of the Académie des Beaux-Arts excluded the young painters from official exhibitions and invited the misunderstanding of the public and critics. As early as the 1863 Salon des Refusés, Manet found himself harshly ridiculed for having dared to exhibit his *Déjeuner sur l'Herbe*. The nudity of the woman bather was all the more shocking because it was unconnected with any mythological theme. The Jury of the 1865 Salon refused the *Olympia* (1863) for similar reasons. Monet, Pissarro and Sisley were generally rejected by the annual Salon in the same way. Now, this rejection at the time was a disaster. As they were unable to exhibit their paintings, the artists found themselves reduced to dire poverty, and forced either to give up their careers or hardly survive at all. Renoir, who lived with his parents, could not afford the necessary paints; Pissarro, married with seven children, always lived in precarious circumstances; Monet, who lived with his mistress and his son, was desperate and really died of hunger. A few art lovers and artists more fortunately placed, like Bazille and Caillebotte, gave them unstinted financial help. Theirs was the first generation of "peintres maudits" (ill-fated painters). Gauguin and Van Gogh followed and their destinies were even more tragic. The eight independent exhibitions of the Impressionists only earned them gibes and hatred. This ostracism was so strong that several years later when they were established, their works met with the same hostile contempt from French museums. In 1896, when Hugo von Tschudi bought a Monet for the Berlin National Gallery, the representatives of the administration, MM. Roujon and Bénédite, gave way to the demands of the members of the Académie des Beaux-Arts, led by the famous Gérôme, and refused half the Caillebotte legacy in 1894/96. He had left sixty-seven Impressionist paintings to the Musée du Luxembourg, bought one by one from his needy friends. It was an unhoped-for opportunity to give a generous representation to the new movement in this museum, yet only forty-two works from the whole collection were accepted and the present Musée du Jeu de Paume lost at one blow the chance to possess three Cézannes, eight Monets and eleven Pissarros. In their impoverished beginnings, the Impressionists could only sell their works in lots at the Hôtel Drouot for ridiculous prices. In 1870, when the collection of their friend and patron, Hoschedé, was broken up, their paintings went for disastrous sums; Monets fetched between 40 and 500 frs. and two Pissarros were given away for 7 and 10 frs. The only support for these artists in their desperate straits came from their dealers, who had faith in them in spite of everything. Durand-Ruel met Monet and Pissarro in London in 1871 and immediately became interested in them. He made the acquaintance of their friends, bought numerous Manets, and welcomed Degas and Sisley to his gallery in 1872, then Renoir in 1873. He held in the rue Le Peletier several group exhibitions of Impressionist paintings, which were very badly received by the public. Then he put on one-man shows for Monet, Renoir, Pissarro and Sisley in 1883, and Renoir in 1892. Later he exhibited them in London, where they had a cool reception, and at New York in 1886, where the three hundred paintings were favourably received. Durand-Ruel built his fortune on the work of these painters, whose genius and tenacity he was the first to appreciate, but he deserved it, because he was forced to take considerable risks to back them up during a period when avant-garde tastes frightened away prospective buyers. Père Tanguy, a little shop-keeper in the rue Clauzel, who had been very helpful to the painters who came to buy colors from him, chose his paintings because he liked them and without a thought of making a profit. Vollard's disinterestedness is less certain, but he had the courage to gamble on the paintings of Cézanne, whom everyone spurned, and gave him a one-man show in 1895. Georges Petit also exhibited the Impressionists and brought together, for example, the works of Monet and Rodin in 1889. With them began the ascendency of the galleries. Whether they cold shouldered or encouraged artists, they were to play the leading rôle in the 20th century to the exclusion of the displaced Salons.

The Galerie du Jeu de Paume houses all the artists, who stood against official art between 1860 and 1890 and suffered badly as a consequence. Although they have certain points in common, they are nevertheless very different from each other.

The painting of Fantin-Latour, who painted in an academic style, gives the first room an intimate atmosphere with nostalgic, lyrical overtones. It is not an accident that this first room should be devoted to his work; he appreciated the importance to painting of his friends' work; he painted their portraits in his big works (*Homage to Delacroix,* 1864; *The Studio at Batignolles,* 1870), perhaps more from admiration for their perseverance and integrity than from acceptance of their aesthetic. He honored them as he honored the poets and critics in *The Corner of the Table.*

The works of painters, like Boudin and Jongkind, who anticipated Impressionism, are gathered together in one room in the gallery. They were the first to paint, in the open air, racing seas, changing skies and beaches scattered with crinolines. Although their treatment of landscape for the sake of its ephemeral effects was modern, it was still tinged with romanticism. Guigou and Bazille made similar experiments on moors burnt with the sun, where they tried to paint the clear skies, sheer rocks and dark trees. Bazille's figures are encircled by this dry, electric atmosphere (*Family Reunion,* 1867/69).

Manet, who was both the predecessor and fellow painter of the Impressionists although very different from them, blazed out in spite of himself the path of revolt and independence that all the young artists were to tread. The hostile reception given to his large works threw him into the company of men whom he influenced profoundly between 1870 and 1876 and gave a taste for open air painting and bright colors. Manet, a unique genius of varied and contradictory qualities, was at the same time a realistic painter (*The Balcony, 1868/69*), the leader of the Impressionists and the first of the Synthetists (*The Fifer,* 1866).

Monet, Sisley, Pissarro and Guillaumin were alone in possessing all the characteristic features of Impressionism: a passion for the study of light, a fondness for open air painting and subjects taken from everyday life, the broken application of color and the rejection of local color. The names of Berthe Morisot and Mary Cassatt can be added to theirs, since they shared their vision of spacious, colored landscape, their way of painting, free from bitumens and unfettered by rules, but they did not give up the art of portraiture. Their portraits of children and serene young women are painted with an acute sensitiveness (Mary Cassatt, *Mother and Child*). As for Renoir, he still kept, along with his allegiance to Impressionism (*Path through Grass,* 1875/77), his attraction to an opulent type of feminine nude, which he was painting at the end of his life in a range of colors resembling the palette of the 18th century (*Bathers,* 1918).

Degas also joined in the rebellious upsurge of the young painters, but he never adopted their way of looking at things nor their technique. Although he was a fine portraitist, he was particularly attracted to painting movement. He was interested in the photographic experiments of Marey and Muybridge on the subject, but photography does not seem to have had as great an influence on him as has been supposed; the novel audacity of the way he placed his subjects only appeared much later in photography. His concern for the study of composition distinguishes him from the rest of the Impressionists, while his incisive draughtsmanship is the opposite to the fluid technique that he only employed at the end of his life when half blind and was using colored cross-hatching for pastels. He had a considerable influence on Toulouse-Lautrec, in so far as he took over the startling effect of Degas' unusual compositions. Lautrec sometimes imitated the juxtaposition of pure color from Impressionism, which he transformed into swift, nervous slashings. Cézanne, living in isolation, attached himself to the impressionist movement, but he always contributed with certain reservations to the exhibitions of a group who gave him a reticent welcome. After a period of expressionistic romanticism (*The Magdalen,* 1866/68), he drew closer to his friends and, like them, preferred to paint nature on the motif (*The House of the Hanged Man,* 1873). However, he pursued a path parallel to theirs in his search for a geometric construction through volume and forms modeled with color (*The Card Players,* 1886). Van Gogh, who was converted to Impressionism during his stay in Paris (*Restaurant de la Sirène,* 1887/88), developed a technique with febrile touches of color, which give his paintings their tormented character. Muted blues are placed beside strident colors and luminous yellows. Van Gogh inherited the technique of the Impressionists and their love of landscape, but he went beyond them in his desperate expressionism. Seurat and Signac, dubbed Neo-impressionists by Fénéon in *L'Art Moderne* in 1886, transcribed Monet's empirical experiments into pictorial formulas and applied scientific theories of light in a systematic method of their own. They were, with Cross, the leaders of the divisionist movement which Pissarro and Van Gogh joined for a brief period. Their paintings possess a deliberate quality and a fine equilibrium of line and color, which are sometimes a little cold (Seurat, *The Circus,* 1891), but their rapid, vital sketches are treated in an Impressionist manner.

The other painters represented in the Jeu de Paume turned away completely from Impressionism; their works are informed with different pictorial aims, which sometimes have literary and religious intentions. Gauguin is the most famous of the Synthesist painters of the Pont-Aven group, which exhibited in 1889 at the Café Volpini and from which the Nabis originated a few years later. In the beginning he was concerned with giving a faithful representation of the subject (*The Seine at the Pont d'Iéna,* 1875), but from this he went on to paint in large areas of flat color, outlined with a firm, black line. The longing to leave home lured him into distant travels that were rather more exotic than the Sunday walks of his friends. He ended his life in the Marquesas Islands, enthralled by the natives whose motionless or incantatory attitudes he painted in intense colors (*And the Gold of their bodies . . . ,* 1901). He also sculptured their hieratic poses in barbaric bas-reliefs, which were taken from his hut at Hiva-Oa and are now exhibited by the museum in a sort of chapel. An inspiration of quite another kind guided Odilon Redon, who was imbued with symbolist philosophy and poetry. Most of his works are evocative of religious mysteries and legendary dreams (*Closed Eyes,* 1890), but he was also a distinguished painter of flowers that are as delicate and strange as his apparitions. The neo-primitivism of the Douanier Rousseau has a similar literary context. The artificial childishness of his style expresses a feeling either of anxious reflection (*War,* 1894) or the fascination of imaginary worlds (*The Snake Charmer,* 1907).

After 1900, the Impressionists were accepted by the public in Europe. Innumerable exhibitions were held in Paris, Brussels, Berlin, London,

Leipzig, and books devoted to their period were published everywhere. The revenge of the "peintres maudits" came when painting in bright colors conquered the academic studios. Then the search for new ways of painting, the Nabis, Cubists and Fauves, unleashed the diatribes of critics against their various aesthetic audacities and Impressionism, imitated and outstripped, found a refuge in the museum.

THÉRÈSE BUROLLET

BAZILLE. THE FAMILY REUNION. 1867.

THE PAINTERS AND THEIR WORK

BAZILLE Jean-Frédéric. Born in Montpellier, 1841; died in Beaune - la - Rolande, 1870. Of the Montpellier upper class, he was still a young man when, at Bruyas' house he saw works by Corot, Delacroix, and Courbet; especially Courbet made a lasting impression on him. After completion of his secondary education, Bazille obtained permission from his liberal-minded parents to go to Paris to continue his medical studies and, at the same time, attend a painter's studio. At Gleyre's, in 1862, he met Monet, Renoir, and Sisley. His wealth enabled him to lead the life of a fashionable young man, and he was always ready to help his less fortunate friends. Monet took him on a holiday to Chailly in the forest of Fontainebleau, and, in 1864, to Honfleur. Inseparable companions, they shared the same studio in Paris.

When Monet found himself in dire straits, Bazille bought the *Women in a Garden* from him for 2,500 francs; true, he paid in monthly installments of 50 francs, but then a student's purse is not inexhaustible. He was the most discreet of friends, always anxious to help, the good companion who both admired and advised the others. When, in the summer of 1870, the outbreak of the Franco-Prussian War took him by surprise in Montpellier, he enlisted in a regiment of Zouaves. He was killed in battle at Beaune-la-Rolande. Because his career was broken off so early, Bazille's works are few, but they show a wealth of promise. Less individual than Monet, but equally gifted, he exerted a marked influence on the latter, and it is not unreasonable to suppose that, had he lived, Impressionism after 1870 might have taken a different course. His two most famous works, *The Family Reunion* and *The Studio,* are reminiscent of Manet in their absence of sculptural qualities, in the similarity of their contrasts, as well as in the rather severe, reserved treatment of composition and color harmonies. A firm, solid, calm style imbues

even those subjects with true grandeur which, reproduced with photographic candor, could easily seem pleasantly banal.

La robe rose, 1864.
Lisière de forêt à Fontainebleau, 1865.
Réunion de famille, 1867.
L'atelier de Bazille, 1870.

BOUDIN Eugène. Born in Honfleur, 1824; died in Deauville, 1898. The importance which Boudin attributed to working in the open air and "to atmospheric conditions, according to the place, time, and wind" (Baudelaire) explains the influence which he exercised on the young Monet and, through him, on the early stages of Impressionism. "It is less this world than the element which envelops it that we reproduce," he said. Originally the proprietor of a small stationery shop in Le Havre, he received encouragement from Millet and, beginning in 1845, he devoted himself to painting. In 1850, a scholarship enabled him to study in Paris for three years. "Everyone expected that after three years I would return a phoenix in the world of art; I came back more perplexed than ever, feeling the pull of the famous figures of those days; from Rousseau who captivated us, to Corot who was beginning to show us a new road. . . . Gray painting was very little appreciated at that time, especially in seascapes. Gudin reigned; Isabey improved on the coloring of nature. Le Poittevin and others created a furore by painting from memory; this was hardly the time to introduce gray. Nobody wanted it. One was forced to retire to one's own countryside and wait for better days, and that is why I went away for fifteen years without returning to Paris." After his return to Le Havre he worked with Jongkind, with the young Monet whom he initiated into painting in 1862, and with Courbet, who freed him from his timidity. He took part in the first Impressionist exhibition (1874) and, late in life, won some official recognition—a gold medal at the International Exhibition (1889) and the Legion of Honor (1892). But all his friends knew his true worth: "If I have become a painter, I owe it to Eugène Boudin" (Monet); "You are the king of skies" (Corot); "You are a seraphim, there is no one but you who knows the sky"

(Courbet). He visited Brittany, Belgium, Holland, and Venice, but for all practical purposes his work rotated around the estuary of the Seine; he loved its silvery beaches, the little ports with their sails outlined against the sky. « How fresh it is: it is soft, faded, slightly rose-tinted. The objects dissolve. There is nothing but color values everywhere. The sea was superb, the sky soft and velvety; it later turned to yellow; it became warm and then the setting sun imbued everything with beautiful nuances of bluish-purple. . ."

La plage de Trouville, 1865.
Plage en Normandie, 1865.
La jetée de Deauville, 1869.
Baigneurs sur la plage de Trou-
  ville, 1869.
Voiliers.
Le port d'Anvers, 1871.
Le port de Bordeaux, 1874.
Étude de ciel.

CAILLEBOTTE G u s t a v e. Born in Paris, 1848; died in Gennevilliers, 1894. His name evokes less a painter than a collector, for his powers of discernment were greater than his talent. He had initially frequented Bonnat's studio, had even been ad.

mitted to the École des Beaux-Arts in 1873, but he was discouraged from the outset and did not continue. Instead, he devoted himself to marine engineering. He lived at Argenteuil. Monet became his neighbor, took him on boating parties with his friends and thus introduced him to the movement. It was Caillebotte whom Renoir painted in profile, astride a chair in the foreground of the *Déjeuner des Canotiers*. Timid and reserved himself, he appreciated audacity in others. For them he was providence itself, always buying "what is unsalable" *(The Swing, Le Moulin de la Galette)* and playing an active part in the organization of their exhibitions. Preoccupied with the fate of his collection—he was a bachelor—he made a will in 1876 which left all his pictures to the state on condition that they be hung in the Louvre. Renoir was named as his executor. On his death in 1894, the conditions of the legacy came under dispute. The scandal was considerable, the Institute indignant. Gérôme, the illustrious painter-member of the Institute, threatened to resign: "I do not know these gentlemen and of the donation I know only the title. . . . Are there not some paintings of Monsieur Monet in it ? Of Monsieur Pissarro and others ? For the state to accept such filth would be a blot on morality." Clemenceau intervened. Renoir came to terms with the state and 8 out of 16 Monets, 7 out of 18 Pissarros, 2 out of 4 Cézannes were accepted; these were finally hung in the Louvre—in 1928.

Les raboteurs de parquet, 1875.
Toits sous la neige, 1878.
Portrait de M. Cordier, 1883.
Voiliers à Argenteuil, *about* 1888.

CASSATT Mary. Born in Pittsburgh, Pa., 1845; died in Mesnil-Beaufresne (Oise), 1926. The daughter of a banker, she went to Europe in 1868 to complete the education she had received at the Pennsylvania Academy and to visit the museums of Italy, Spain, and Belgium. Very well informed on the world of art, she advised her friend Mrs. Havemeyer to buy the works of Degas. He, who did not know her, noticed her work in the 1874 Salon. A mutual friend introduced them, and this meeting marked the beginning of a deep friendship; for the first time, Degas

abandoned his misogyny. They shared the feelings common to the class to which they belonged, and yet they had the same scorn for convention. Both were cooly rational, and both preferred drawing to color. At the age of thirty-two, prompted by her desire to break away from the social obligations imposed by her environment as well as by her feeling of artistic vocation, Mary Cassatt devoted herself entirely to painting. She follow-ed the advice of Degas, but the simplification and precision of her line are more reminiscent of Japanese prints. She was an Impressionist in her use of colors and also in the treatment of her themes of motherhood and infancy, of which she painted innumerable series. Living in the heart of the Impressionist movement, she contributed con-siderably toward making the works of her friends known in America. When Durand-Ruel found himself on the brink of bankruptcy because of the concerted efforts of his fellow art dealers, she lent him money. She bought Impressionist paintings both for herself and for her family and made her other friends —the Havemeyers of New York, the Stillmans, and the Whittemores—buy them. Practically blind, she died in her Château at Mesnil-Beaufresne near Beauvais.

Femme cousant, *about* 1886.
Mère et enfant.

CÉZANNE Paul. Born in Aix-en-Provence, 1839; died there, 1906. After establishing a comfortable business in the hat trade, his father had become a prosperous banker. Cézanne's career, therefore, seemed mapped out in advance; after a normal secondary education at the Aix lycée, where he made friends with his fellow pupil Zola, he began to study law. But his feeling for art was overwhelming, and though it was not in line with the plans of his father, he was finally allowed to leave for Paris in 1861. There he enrolled at the Académie Suisse, sought the company of Pissarro, and strove to get into the École des Beaux-Arts. Oddly enough, the reason for his rejection was: "Cézanne has the temperament of a colorist. Unfortunately, he paints with violence." Cézanne had looked forward to the reestablishment of the close ties with his old friend Zola, and the increasing coolness of their relationship added to his feeling of dejection. Mortified and helpless, Cézanne returned to Aix. His father made every effort to interest him in his banking business, but on one of the ledgers the young Paul wrote these lines: "Cézanne the banker shudders at what he sees—behind his counter a future painter is being born." Tired of fighting, his father again agreed to send his son to Paris in November, 1862. At the Académie Suisse he found Pissarro once more and was introduced to Guillaumin, Degas, Bazille, Monet, Renoir, and Sisley. But his shyness and modesty made him adopt an expression of fierceness and he made friends only with some difficulty. Also, the power, vehemence, and baroque quality of his painting left people aghast. He was refused a second time at

CÉZANNE. THE HOUSE OF THE HANGED MAN. 1873.

the École des Beaux-Arts (1863) and rejected by the Salon (1866). Paris oppressed him, and during the course of these years he often escaped to Aix to recuperate in the land that suited his fiery temperament so well. He worked extremely hard, nearly always in solitude; he had to teach himself everything, to discover everything, and these self-imposed difficulties exasperated him.

When war broke out in 1870, he remained at Estaque, near Marseille, and devoted himself to landscape painting. But the course of events had dispersed his friends and, after the war, rather than return to Paris, he preferred to set himself up in Auvers-sur-Oise, where Pissarro was then living.

His stay in Auvers (1872-1874) proved decisive. Alongside Pis-

CÉZANNE. L'ESTAQUE. 1882-1885.

sarro, he acquired the discipline which had been so lacking, the economy of means and the equilibrium necessary for inspiration and execution. Converted to Impressionism, he took up painting in the open air; his palette became brighter, his touch was no longer heavy, as if laid on with the knife, but restrained, regular, and delicate. His logical mind, however, demanded a greater discipline than the pseudo-analytical approach of Monet. He aspired toward a more synthecized and constructive vision, of which the basic elements would be the sphere, the cylinder, and the cone. He made contact again with his painter friends and, in 1874, participated in their first exhibition at Nadar's, where he showed three pictures, including the *Modern Olympia* and *The*

House of the Hanged Man. At the exhibition which the Impressionist group organized three years later (1877) in the Rue Le Peletier, he was represented by sixteen canvases; but, hurt by the hilarity they provoked, he returned to the solitude of his native countryside, determined "to make of Impressionism something solid and lasting, like the art of museums." Each year he made an appearance in Paris so as not to be forgotten, hoping that at some time he might finally be able to win over the jury. Thanks to the charitable intervention of Guillemet, he was at last able to announce to this family that he had been accepted for the Salon of 1882. But he was aware of the insignificance of this encouragement and, tired of the machinations and intrigues of the Parisian art world, be retired to Aix, relinquishing the pursuit

CÉZANNE. STILL-LIFE WITH ONIONS. 1895-1900.

of success and, at the same time, that superficial search after fugitive effects which satisfied his Impressionist friends. For at heart, Cézanne, the man of the Mediterranean, was a classicist. Impressionism had burst the bonds of official painting and had rediscovered the vitality of a true tradition. It had, above all, discovered light, and Cézanne never disowned this fundamental contribution. But he meant to go beyond it, to deepen his sensation. He did not want to sacrifice volume and space, but, on the contrary, to accentuate them in simplifying them, and, finally, he wished to achieve the harmony of color within that of form.

After 1889, success arrived slowly. At the International Exhibition he was able to show *The House of the Hanged Man ;* the following year he was invited to exhibit in Brussels. In 1895, Vollard exhibited some 150 works in his shop in the Rue Laffitte. This created a scandal, but Cézanne became aware of the admiration he excited among young painters and young critics— Maurice Denis, Émile Bernard, Gasquet, Jaloux, and Larguier— and his art blossomed under this approval. Going beyond the geometric synthesis of previous years, he gave himself up to lyricism of form and color which he strove to integrate into his vision of reality. It was a difficult task, by no means lacking in obstacles; it postulated a perfect sincerity with regard to reality as well as with regard to himself. A few days before his death, he was able to write to Émile Bernard: "I am always studying, and it seems to me that I am making slow progress." The retrospective exhibition of 1907 in the Salon d'Automne with 56 canvases from the Pellerin, Cézanne, and Gangnat collections, was an affirmation of Cézanne's triumph. The Louvre had received some of his works through the Camondo bequest and these were exhibited there in 1911.

Tête de vieillard, *about* 1865/68.

La Madeleine ou la Douleur, *about* 1866/68.

Une moderne Olympia, *vers* 1873.

La maison du Docteur Gachet, *vers* 1873.

Pommes vertes, *about* 1873.

Bouquet au dahlia jaune, *about* 1873.

Nature morte au médaillon Solari, *about* 1873.

CÉZANNE. THE BLUE VASE. 1885-1887.

Carrefour de la rue Rémy à Auvers, *about* 1873.

La maison du pendu, 1873.

Bouquet au petit Delft, *about* 1873/75.

Dahlias, 1875.

Le pont de Maincy, dit le petit pont, 1879.

Cour de ferme à Auvers, *about* 1879/80.

Les peupliers, *about* 1879/82.

Portrait de l'artiste par lui-même, *about* 1880/81.

L'Estaque, *about* 1882/85.

Nature morte à la soupière, *about* 1883/85.

Le vase bleu, *about* 1885/87.

Les joueurs de cartes, *about* 1885/90.

Nature morte au panier, *about* 1888/90.

Baigneurs, *about* 1890/94.

La femme à la cafetière, *about* 1890/94.

Nature morte aux oignons, *about* 1895/1900.

Pommes et oranges, *about* 1895/1900.

DEGAS Edgar. Born in Paris, 1834; died there, 1917. "The air that one can see in the work of the old masters is not the air that one breathes." "My art is in no way spontaneous; it is entirely contrived." Thus Degas, who had played a part in the advent of Impressionism, stood opposed to two basic principles of the movement—the necessity of, or almost superstitious belief in, open-air painting, and direct impression. This affirmation of independence, or, more exactly, his rejection of the approval of others, constituted the drama of his life and work. His father was a banker and Degas, free to direct his life as he chose, decided after an excellent classical education to devote himself to painting and went through his apprenticeship at the École des Beaux-Arts (1855). But he would not allow himself to be tied down, and the following year he left for Italy to study the Florentine masters (1856-1860). The works dating from this period not only show the influence of the Italian sixteenth-century masters, but also a heightened and already individual vision. His feeling for composition and for spontaneous movement led him to the group of painters of the Café Guerbois, and more particularly to Manet, whom he had met in the Louvre. Between them there sprang up a close friendship, often stormy but firmly anchored, which led

DEGAS. AT THE RACES. 1869-1872.

to a sort of emulation in the choice and utilization of themes borrowed from everyday life: racetracks and café scenes; women washing themselves, brushing their hair, women bathing — themes in which Degas usually found fresh approaches. For it was the unusual motif as much as the original arrangement of the picture that he looked for, as in the *Racecourse* series (begun in 1862), the *Theater* series (begun in 1868), and his ballet pictures, all subjects which were still completely novel. Degas took part in the first Impressionist exhibition in 1874, but he was the only one among them who sacrificed none of the precision of an uncompromising vision, the only one, also, who considered drawing to be the means of expression which best reconciled his love of movement with his love of precision: "I paint with the line." But, para-doxically, when his eyesight deteriorated he was to translate his inner vision in accents of intense color—blues, yellows, and reds—in powerfully juxta-posed brush strokes. He was a perpetual inventor of new techniques, and when threatened with total blindness he gave up pastels for sculpture (*The Little Dancer Aged Fourteen* was shown at the Impressionist exhibition of 1881). Difficult and independent as he was, he gave his support to Impressionism, yet he remain-ed practically a stranger to the movement. He was the first person to buy a Gauguin and so, to some extent, the sponsor of

DEGAS.
ABSINTHE.
1876.

DEGAS. DANCER ON THE STAGE. *c.* 1878.

DEGAS. THE LAUNDRESSES. *c.* 1884.

the man who was to signal the end of Impressionism. His superior intelligence, his logical and mocking mind, and his intractable character were just as responsible for his isolation as was his infirmity. There remained to him the bitter consolation of being alone among the Ingres, the Delacroix, and the Cézannes of his collection.

Portrait de l'artiste, *about* 1854/55.

Portrait de Giovannina Bellelli, *about* 1856.

Portrait de Hilaire-René de Gas, 1857.

Portrait de Marguerite de Gas, *about* 1858/60

Portrait de Marguerite de Gas, *vers* 1858/60.

Sémiramis construisant Babylone, 1861.

La famille Bellelli, *vers* 1858/60.
Course de gentlemen, avant le départ, 1862.
Portrait de Thérèse de Gas, duchesse Morbilli, 1863.
Degas et Valernes, *vers* 1864.
Les malheurs de la ville d'Orléans, 1865.
Portrait de jeune femme, 1867.
Études de mains, *vers* 1868.

Portrait de Valernes, 1868.
Le violoncelliste Pillet, *vers* 1868/69.
Les musiciens à l'orchestre, *vers* 1868/69.
Portraits de Pagans et d'Auguste de Gas, *vers* 1869.
Au bord de la mer, *vers* 1869.
Chevaux de courses, devant les tribunes, *vers* 1869/72.

DEGAS.
WOMAN COMBING
HER HAIR.
c. 1887-1890.

Portrait de Mlle Dihau au piano, *about* 1869/71.

Portraits de Jeantaud, Linet et Lainé, 1871.

Blanchisseuses souffrant des dents, *about* 1870/72.

La femme à la potiche, 1872.

Le foyer de la danse à l'Opéra de la rue Le Peletier, 1872.

Le pédicure, 1873.

Répétition d'un ballet sur la scène, 1874.

La classe de danse, 1874.

L'absinthe, 1876.

Femmes à la terrasse d'un café, 1877.

Fin d'arabesque, 1877.

Choristes : les figurants, 1877.

Femme sortant du bain, 1877.

Aux courses, jockeys amateurs, *about* 1877/80.

Danseuse au bouquet, saluant, 1878.

L'étoile, 1878.

A la Bourse, *about* 1878/79.

Femme nue accroupie de dos, *about* 1879.

Danseuse assise nouant son brodequin, *about* 1881/83.

Femme dans son bain s'épongeant la jambe, *about* 1883.

Les repasseuses, *about* 1884.

Le café-concert, 1885.

Le tub, 1886.

Après le bain, femme s'essuyant les pieds, 1886.

Danseuses montant un escalier, *about* 1886/90.

Femme se coiffant, *about* 1887/90.

Danseuses bleues, *about* 1890.

Deux baigneuses sur l'herbe, *about* 1890/95.

Femme se lavant dans sa baignoire, *about* 1892.

Après le bain, femme s'essuyant le cou, 1898.

Chanteuse.

FANTIN-LATOUR Théodore. Born in Grenoble in 1836, died at Buré (Orne) in 1904. His family was of Italian origin and his mother was Russian. He received artistic training at a very early age, for his father was a painter and teacher of drawing, and while still a boy, left Grenoble for Paris. Together with Legros, he studied under Lecocq de Boisbaudran before spending a short time at the studio of Courbet, who rejected him. He worked a great deal in the Louvre where he made copies after paintings by Watteau, Veronese, Van Dyck and Poussin, and became friendly with the future Impressionists who met in his studio in the Rue des Beaux-Arts and then at the Café Guerbois (about 1868). He became a friend of Manet, whose portrait he paint-

FANTIN-LATOUR.
NARCISSI
AND TULIPS.
1862.

ed (1867), and Whistler, who influenced him and invited him to England (1859, 1861, 1864). Although he was to be allowed to exhibit at the Salon, he also took part in the Salon des Refusés in 1863, where he exhibited a *Féerie*.

Fantin-Latour did not share his revolutionary fellow-artists' sensitivity to light and was only interested in realism and modernity for a short time. Although he is mostly known for his large collective portraits which renewed the genre (*Homage to Delacroix,* 1864; *The Studio in the Batignolles,* 1870; *The Corner of the Table,* 1872; *Around the Piano,* 1885) and his flower paintings (about 1872-1874), he became increasingly interested in painting "visions of visions" (G. Kahn). It was music especially that inspired his numerous but unadventurous lithographs, dating from 1890 onwards (Schumann, Berlioz, Wagner, Brahms) but his finest work dates from before the Symbolist movement, in the years between 1860 and 1880, when his art had not yet become subordinated to his theories, and was still the sincerest expression of his poetic talent.

La liseuse (Marie Fantin-Latour), 1861.
Narcisses et tulipes, 1862.
Hommage à Delacroix, 1864.
Fleurs, 1865.
Esquisse de l'atelier des Batignolles, *about* 1870.
L'atelier des Batignolles, 1870.
Un coin de table, 1872.
Portrait de Mme Fantin-Latour, 1873.
Les trois Filles du Rhin, 1876.
La famille Dubourg, 1878.
Portrait de Charlotte Dubourg, 1882.
Autour du piano, 1885.
Portrait d'Adolphe Jullien, 1887.
Étude de femme nue.
Le coucher.
La Nuit, 1897.

GAUGUIN Paul. Born in Paris, 1848; died in Atuana in the Marquesas Islands, 1903. His father was a journalist of Radical Republican convictions; his mother, born in Peru, was the daughter of the painter André Chazan and of a Spanish mother—Flora Tristan, a militant disciple of Saint-Simon and a woman of letters. Through her, he was descended from the Borgias d'Aragon, who had been viceroys of Peru. After the *coup d'état* of 1851, the Gauguin family went into voluntary exile to Lima. Gauguin's mother, having lost her husband, returned to France with her children after spending four years in Peru. Paul was then aged seven. Educated in Orléans, he was attracted to the life of a sailor. He enlisted as an apprentice on a merchant ship, visited Rio de Janeiro, Bahia, Sweden, and Denmark. After the death of his mother in 1871 he gave up the sea and became a broker. In 1873, he married a young Danish woman, Mette-Sophie Gad. He had a fine bourgeois household, five children, social life, money. But one of the employees of the bank, a man by the name of Schuffenecker, used to devote his spare time to painting and induced Gauguin to follow his example: it was an agreeable Sunday pastime which

GAUGUIN. TAHITIAN WOMEN. 1891.

came to absorb him more and more. He showed a landscape at the Salon of 1876 and slowly amassed pictures by Jongkind, Manet, Renoir, Monet, Pissarro, and Sisley. He spent 15,000 francs on building up a collection of Impressionist works. Pissarro advised him and introduced him to Cézanne as well as to the rest of the group. Gauguin exhibited with them on several occasions. He was still looked on as an amateur but, in the autumn of 1883, he gave up the bank and moved with his wife and children to Rouen where Pissarro lived. Full of ambition, he assumed that his work would enable him to lead a life of ease. But he sold nothing, and his savings were soon exhausted. His wife became exasperated and, worn out, took him to Denmark in 1884 in the hope of bringing him back to an outlook more in conformity with the bourgeois norm. An exhibition in Copenhagen was a failure; Gauguin abandoned his family, except for his son Clovis, and returned to Paris in 1885. To keep himself alive he became a billposter.

Soon afterwards, escaping from the city, he went to Brittany in 1886, and took up residence at an inn in Pont-Aven frequented by painters from the Cormon studio and the Académie Julian. There he kept to himself, a focal point of curiosity for all. When he returned to Paris, he made friends with Van Gogh, visited Degas, and planned a trip to the

GAUGUIN.
THE WHITE HORSE.
1898.

GAUGUIN. AREAREA. 1892.

tropics. In the spring of 1887, he embarked for Martinique, but returned the following year, completely penniless, and once more took refuge in Pont-Aven. Then, summoned by Van Gogh, he went to Arles. But the visit to Provence ended tragically and Gauguin returned to Paris. At the Café Volpini his work was included in "An Exhibition of Paintings of the Impressionist and Synthesist Groups" and he exhibited in Brussels with *Les Vingt*. In 1891, he left for Tahiti to live "in ecstasy, in peace, and in art," and strove to rid himself of everything that was not elemental. "For me, Barbary is a restorer of youth." In 1893, he exhibited his Tahitian works at Durand-Ruel's; they created considerable interest, particularly among the younger generation—

Bonnard, Vuillard, and the Nabis. Having broken with the Impressionists, he returned to Tahiti in 1895, lived his legend and, despite illness, misery, and ridiculous squabbles with the local authorities, never stopped producing masterpieces. Penniless and embittered, his health completely broken, he died in the Marquesas Islands on May 8, 1903.

La Seine au pont d'Iéna, 1875.
Nature morte à la mandoline, 1885.
La fenaison en Bretagne, 1888.
Les Alyscamps, 1888.
La famille Schuffenecker, 1889.
La belle Angèle, 1889.
Nature morte à l'éventail, *about* 1889.
Femmes de Tahiti sur la plage, 1891.
Areara, 1892.
Paysage de Bretagne, 1894.
Vairumati, 1897.
Le cheval blanc, 1898.
Et l'or de leur corps, 1901.
Village breton sous la neige, *about* 1894, retouched 1903.

GONZALÈS Éva. Born in Paris, 1849; died there, 1883. She came of a cultured background, receptive to the arts, and it was only natural that her family, becoming aware of her talent, should put her under the tutelage of the painter Chaplin. Her small studio in the Rue Bréda was near Manet's, which was then giving rise to a certain amount of talk. Famous men surrounded by an aura of scandal exercise a fascinating attraction on innocent young ladies. Alfred Stevens, a friend of the Gonzalès', introduced Manet to them. Éva became his pupil and worked assiduously in close contact with him during 1869. She adopted his mannerisms, and her painting might almost be said to be a poeticized version of Manet. She learned to simplify and to reject everything that was not essential. But she stiffened instinctively in the face of Impressionism. Her obstinacy was undoubtedly due in part to the fact that Manet was introduced to the new theories by another charming young woman who might have proved a rival. But she did not. Berthe Morisot married Eugène Manet, and Éva Gonzalès married their mutual friend Henri Guérard, a collector of etchings. He, who lived on the fringe of the movement and was more concerned with his collection than with living art, no doubt warned his young wife against all modernist tendencies. At the 1879 Salon, she exhibited a number of canvases which affirmed her taste for interior scenes. But was she aware of being on the wrong track? She seemed to return to Impressionism, used both more lively colors and a bolder touch. She died in childbirth, at the age of thirty-four.

La nichée, ou la matinée rose.
Une loge aux Italiens, *about* 1874.

GUILLAUMIN Armand. Born in Paris, 1841; died there, 1927. "He· is an architect of the great future ahead and a good fellow of whom I am very fond," said Cézanne. The two men had met at the Académie Suisse through Pissarro, and they formed a little group which always remained united. Forced to earn his living as an employee of the railways, Guillaumin devoted his free Sundays to painting and often went to Auvers-sur-Oise to join his friends gathered at the house of Doctor Gachet. He took part in the first Impressionist exhibition in 1874 and remained one of the few faithfuls whose work was still to be seen at the last exhibition of 1886. He was, in fact, immune to external influences and thus preserved his very direct and personal vision. In 1891, he won a 100,000 franc prize in a lottery which enabled him to devote his time entirely to painting. His landscapes of the Creuse and Holland (1904) give an impression of virile authority, an illusion created by the intensity of color, but one which did not always succeed in concealing a lack of discipline.

Chemin creux, effet de neige, 1869.
Péniches sur la Seine, à Bercy, 1871.
Nature morte, 1872.
Soleil couchant à Ivry, *about* 1873.
Portrait de l'artiste, *about* 1870/75.
Nu couché, *about* 1877.
Intérieur, 1889.
Portrait de fillette, 1894.

JONGKIND Johan Barthold. Born in Latrop, Holland, 1819; died in La Côte-Sainte-André, near Grenoble, 1891. The eighth child of a Dutch pastor, Jongkind met the landscape painter Isabey at The Hague; Isabey took him as a pupil and, in 1846, sent him to Paris to complete his studies. A bohemian to the core, an alcoholic, always in debt, he suffered from a feeling of persecution. In 1858, he gained some measure of stability when, in Paris, he met a Dutch woman who helped him and took him with her on her visits to Nivernais and La Côte-Saint-André in the Dauphiné. Heedless of everything which did not immediately satisfy his instinctive genius, his work was uneven, hasty, and disappointing. His oil paintings at their best are in the tradition of the great Dutch landscape painters—Ruysdael and Van Goyen in particular. Nevertheless, this was not enough to make him an Impressionist, any more than the fact that he was one of the first foreign painters of the School of Paris. But his water colors and his drawings are a completely different matter: able to capture the most fleeting of sensations, he had that rapidity of execution and sureness of touch which the Impressionists in turn strove to attain.

Ruines du château de Rosemont, 1861.
En Hollande, les barques près du moulin, 1868.

MANET Édouard. Born in Paris, 1832; died there, 1883. The son of a well-to-do family,

he was sent to boarding school in Vaugirard in 1839, and then to the Collège Rollin, completing his secondary education in 1848. Then he had to choose a career. "You will study law," his father said. But Manet wanted to be a painter. It then was decided that he was to become a naval officer, and he went to sea as an apprentice sailor. A voyage to Rio de Janeiro did not change Manet's mind about his artistic vocation. His father gave way and Édouard enrolled at the studio of Thomas Couture in 1850, where, despite the incompatibility of master and pupil, he remained for nearly six years. From his liaison with Suzanne Leenhoff was born a son, Léon Édouard (1852). In 1863, after the death of his father, Manet married her. His was the easygoing life of a well-off young man and he visited Holland, Germany, and Italy in 1856. The first picture he submitted to the Salon of 1859—the *Absinthe Drinker*—was rejected; but in 1861, the *Spanish Guitar Player* was accepted and given honorable mention. However, the official career of which he dreamed was closed to him. *Lola de Valence, jeune Femme Couchée en Costume Espagnol*

MANET. LE DÉJEUNER SUR L'HERBE. 1863.

and *Concert in the Tuileries Gardens,* all of which were exhibited at Martinet's in 1863, caused a scandal. At the *Salon des Refusés,* the *Déjeuner sur l'Herbe* was taken as a gesture of defiance. It was almost certainly in order to appease the jury that Manet, in the years following, sent in the *Angels at the Tomb of Christ* and *Christ Insulted by the Soldiers,* but he again compromised himself with his *Olympia* (1865). The critics vented their wrath and, despite the congratulations of Baudelaire, Manet, discouraged, went off to Spain. The hostility of the general public and the ostracism of the jury had made him the leader of a school despite himself, and official honors were henceforth out of the question. At the time of the International Exhibition of 1867 he

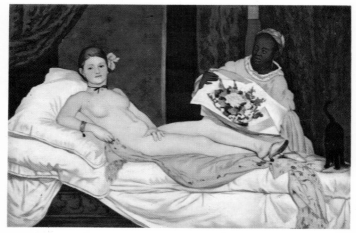

MANET. OLYMPIA. 1863.

had a pavilion erected at his own expense in the Place de l'Alma; there he showed all his rejected canvases. In 1868, however, the Salon accepted the *Portrait of Zola* and the following year the *Déjeuner à l'Atelier* and *The Balcony*. Manet's family was dispersed by the war, and he himself enlisted as a lieutenant in the General Staff of the National Guard. After the end of the war he set himself up in the Rue de Saint-Pétersbourg, where his studio became a meeting-place for his friends: Mallarmé, Antonin Proust, Chabrier, Clemenceau, and pretty young women.

He refused to take part in the Impressionist exhibition at Nadar's in 1874, but, under the influence of his pupil Berthe Morisot (who had become his sister-in-law), he allowed himself to be taken to Gennevilliers and to Argenteuil where he painted *The Monet Family in the Garden*. He seemed to have been won over to the Impressionist aesthetic and it was in this style that he painted the *Grand Canal* of Venice in 1875. The Salon turned him down in 1876 and 1877, when he submitted *Le Linge* and *Nana*. In 1878, he proposed naïvely to the Prefect of the Seine to paint a series of compositions on the theme of Paris—the market, railways, and the Métro. However,

MANET.
THE FIFER.
1866.

MANET. THE BALCONY. 1868-1869.

MANET.
PORTRAIT
OF IRMA BRUNNER.
c. 1882.

struck down by locomotor ataxy, he was forced to pay attention to his health; he took a cure at Bellevue, stayed at Versailles, and worked on *Le Bar aux Folies-Bergère* (1881). But illness undermined his strength and, on April 30, 1883, he died. He had never really known the glory which he craved—a glory amply confirmed by his posthumous exhibition at the École des Beaux-Arts in 1884.

Lola de Valence, 1862.
Le déjeuner sur l'herbe, 1863.
Olympia, 1863.
Fruits sur une table, 1864.
Anguille et rouget, *about* 1864.
Tige de pivoines et sécateur, *about* 1864.
Branche de pivoines blanches et sécateur, *about* 1864.
Vase de pivoines sur piédouche, *about* 1864/65.
Angelina, *about* 1865.
Le fifre, 1866.

Mme Édouard Manet au piano,
about 1868.

Portrait d'Émile Zola, 1868.

La lecture, *about* 1868.

Le balcon, *about* 1868/69.

Clair de lune sur le port de Boulogne, 1869.

Berthe Morisot à l'éventail, 1874.

La dame aux éventails, Nina de Caillas, *about* 1873/74.

Mlle de Conflans, *about* 1875/77.

Mme Manet sur un canapé bleu, 1874 ou 1878.

Portrait de Stéphane Mallarmé, 1876.

La blonde aux seins nus, *about* 1878.

Jeune femme blonde aux yeux bleus, *about* 1878.

La serveuse de bocks, *about* 1878/79.

Portrait de Mme Émile Zola, *about* 1879/80.

Portrait de Clemenceau, *about* 1879/80.

Le citron, *about* 1880.

Portrait de Jean de Cabanes, dit Cabaner, 1880.

Étude de femme nue, en buste, 1880.

Portrait du Dr Materne, 1880.

Œillets et clématites dans un vase de cristal, *about* 1882.

Portrait d'Irma Brunner, *about* 1882.

MONET Claude. Born in Paris, 1840; died in Giverny, 1926. The son of Le Havre shopkeepers, by the time he was fifteen he was already well known for his caricatures; his portrait-caricatures sold for twenty francs apiece and caught the attention of Boudin (1858). The latter's influence was decisive, and on his advice Monet went to Paris in 1859, where, for a short while, he worked at the Académie Suisse with Pissarro; but most of his time was spent in discussions at the Brasserie des Martyrs. Conscripted in 1860, he spent two years in Algeria; but a bout of typhoid fever cut short his military service. He rejoined Boudin and Jongkind at Le Havre, then returned to Paris in 1862 to enroll in the studio of Gleyre, where he made friends with Bazille, Renoir, and Sisley. His love of independence revolted against the formalism of the École and he took his friends with him to Chailly in the forest of Fontainebleau (1863), and to Honfleur (1864). Together they discovered the peaceful horizons of the Ile-de-France, the charm of the banks of the Seine and they frequently escaped into Normandy. At the

MONET. REGATTA AT ARGENTEUIL. *c.* 1872.

Salon of 1866 he exhibited the portrait of *Camille,* but he was not as successful with the *Women in a Garden,* which was rejected by the jury of the 1867 Salon. His material situation was precarious. Tempted to commit suicide, it was the friendship of Bazille which saw him through, despite a new setback at the 1869 Salon. When war was declared he went first to Trouville, then to London, where he found Pissarro once more and made the acquaintance of Durand-Ruel. He then went to Holland, where his landscapes acquired his typical luminous colors.

On his return he went to live in Argenteuil, where, in 1873, he built himself a studio boat like Daubigny's "Botin" from which he could observe the incessant interplay of light and water. He again took up the project which Bazille had envisaged of grouping friends into a society and of giving a joint exhibition of their work. This took place in 1874, at Nadar's, and Monet showed his *Impression, Sunrise.* This exhibit was the official baptism of Impressionism, and Monet was recognized as the leader of the group. But financial

MONET. BRIDGE AT ARGENTEUIL. 1874.

difficulties continued and he lived on loans. Perhaps inspired by Turner, Monet was fascinated by themes which had never been touched before, such as the Gare Saint-Lazare, the railway bridge at Argenteuil, the banks of the Seine at Vétheuil, sacrificing the subject to a study of the changing effects of light. In 1883, he went to live permanently in Giverny, though he still went on visits to Bordighera with Renoir (1884), to Haarlem, to Belle-Ile-en-Mer (1886), to Antibes (1888) and elsewhere. From 1890 until the end of his life he was preoccupied with a variety of themes on which he worked unceasingly. During this period, he produced those amazing series which are the affirmation of all his visionary talent; the *Haystacks* (1890); the *Poplars,* followed by the *Cathedrals* (1893-1894); and then, between 1901 and 1904, the *Water Lilies* and the *Banks of the Thames* ; and finally, in 1908, the *Views of Venice*. Having retired to Giverny, the supreme master of Impressionism died in 1926, having been a part both of its triumph and of its ultimate decline.

Coin d'atelier, 1861.
Trophée de chasse, 1862.
Nature morte, 1864.
Cour de ferme en Normandie, *about* 1864.

MONET.
ROUEN
CATHEDRAL
AND THE TOUR
D'ALBANE,
MORNING EFFECT.
1894.

Route du Bas-Bréau, 1865.

Fragment du Déjeuner sur l'herbe, *about* 1865/66.

La charrette, route sous la neige à Honfleur, *about* 1865/67.

Jardin en fleurs, *about* 1866.

Femmes au jardin, 1867.

Portrait de Mme Gaudibert, 1868.

Train dans la campagne, *about* 1870/71.

Zaandam, 1871.

Chasse-marée à l'ancre, *about* 1871.

Portrait de Mme Monet, *about* 1871.

Régates à Argenteuil, *about* 1872.

Vue de plaine à Argenteuil, 1872.

Carrières-Saint-Denis, 1872.

Les coquelicots, 1873.

Grosse mer à Étretat, *about* 1873.

Bateaux de plaisance, *about* 1873.

Le pont du chemin de fer à Argenteuil, *about* 1873.

Repos sous les lilas, *about* 1873.

Le déjeuner, *about* 1872/74.

Les barques, régates à Argenteuil, 1874.

Le pont d'Argenteuil, 1874.

Les Tuileries, 1875.

Un coin d'appartement, 1875.

Le bassin d'Argenteuil, 1875.

La gare Saint-Lazare, 1877.

Les dindons, 1877.

Chrysanthèmes, 1878.

Église de Vétheuil, neige, 1878/79.

Vétheuil, 1879.

La Seine à Vétheuil, effet de soleil après la pluie, 1879.

La Seine à Vétheuil, *about* 1879/82.

Le givre, 1880.

La Seine à Port-Villez, 1883.

Les rochers de Belle-Ile, 1886.

Tempête, côtes de Belle-Ile, 1886.

Champs de tulipes en Hollande, 1886.

Femme à l'ombrelle, tournée vers la droite, 1886.

Femme à l'ombrelle, tournée vers la gauche, 1886.

La barque à Giverny, 1887.

La cathédrale de Rouen, temps gris, 1894.

La cathédrale de Rouen, soleil matinal, 1894.

La cathédrale de Rouen, le portail et la tour d'Albane, effet du matin, 1894.

La cathédrale de Rouen, le portail et la tour d'Albane, plein soleil, 1894.

La cathédrale de Rouen, 1894.

Bras de Seine près de Giverny, 1897.

Le bassin aux nymphéas, harmonie verte, 1899.

Le bassin aux nymphéas, harmonie rose, 1900.

Vétheuil, soleil couchant, 1901.

MONET. WOMAN WITH A SUNSHADE. 1886.

Etang aux nymphéas, 1904.
Londres, le Parlement, trouée
de soleil dans le brouillard, 1904.
Portrait de l'artiste par lui-même,
1917.

MORISOT Berthe. Born in
Bourges, 1841; died in Paris,
1895. Her well-to-do father was
a prefect under Louis-Philippe.
The bourgeois tradition made
allowances for everything except
for genius. However, Berthe
Morisot, without in any way
renouncing her background or
her deepest aspirations, succeed-
ed in being both a perfect house-
wife and a painter. When she
was fifteen, she and her sister
began to take drawing lessons.
This was part of a young girl's
education and her family was
pleased with the approbation of
her professors. Full of ambition,
she went to work in the Louvre,
studying Raphael, and there she
met Fantin-Latour and Manet,
who made her aware of the
inadequacy of her teaching. She
then studied with Corot, who
was amazed at her talent and lent
her canvases to copy. She exhibited at the Salon of 1864.
But it was Manet who revealed
her to herself. He asked her
to pose for *The Balcony,* and

through him she discovered that a
picture must be built up by means
of rhythm, calculation, and selec-
tion. She realized that her art
was superficial even if the touch
was inspired; therefore she started
painting portraits, which demand
a greater discipline. There are
unquestionable similarities between the work of Berthe Morisot and that of Manet, but this is
due more to a similarity of subject
than to any real influence. The
master, who was so susceptible to
feminine charm, acknowledged
the ascendancy of his pupil, and his
palette, which was still somber,
became more luminous under her
influence.

After 1872, Berthe Morisot's
style broadened and achieved its
equilibrium in a true harmony of
color and light. In 1874 she married Eugène Manet, the handsome,
bearded talker of the *Déjeuner sur
l'Herbe.* Freed by marriage from
the constraining bonds of family
prejudice, she gave up striving
after official approbation and
exhibited at Nadar's in the first
Impressionist exhibition. Renoir,
Mallarmé, Degas, Monet, Caillebotte, and Whistler were all welcome at her home. Her subjects
belonged to her own peaceful
world—the faces of children, inte-

PISSARRO. CHESTNUT TREES AT LOUVECIENNES. 1870.

riors, and open-air scenes. After 1884, her stylistic evolution proceeded logically toward a more generous and firmer treatment of line. She was deeply stricken by her husband's death in 1892 and her work began to suffer. She developed a broader style, less firm and well-constructed. Light suffused form and dissolved it. In the case of Berthe Morisot, this prime weakness of Impressionism was intensified by a feminine sensibility.

Portrait de Mme Pontillon, sœur de l'artiste, 1871.
La chasse aux papillons, 1873.
Le berceau, 1873.
Jeune femme en toilette de bal, *about* 1879/80.
L'hortensia, 1894.

PISSARRO Camille Jacob. Born in Saint-Thomas in the West Indies, 1830; died in Paris, 1903. Sent to Paris to study at the age of twelve, he afterwards

PISSARRO. ENTRANCE TO THE VILLAGE OF VOISINS. 1872.

returned to the West Indies to work in his father's hardware business; ultimately, his family accepted the fact that he wanted to be an artist and permitted him to return to Paris. He arrived there at the time of the 1855 International Exhibition and discovered Ingres, Delacroix, Courbet, and Corot; it was the last-named who exerted a decisive influence upon Pissarro. In 1859, at the Académie Suisse, he met Monet and, two years later, Cézanne and Guillaumin. In 1866 he went to live in Pontoise, and in 1869 he established himself at Louveciennes. In 1870, in face of the Prussian advance, he fled to Brittany and then to London, where he married Julie Vellay, the mother of his children.

PISSARRO. RED ROOFS. 1877.

There he also met Durand-Ruel, who bought two of his canvases, and Monet, who, like himself, was a refugee. When he returned to Louveciennes, the Prussians had ransacked his studio and destroyed nearly fifteen hundred canvases. From 1872 to 1884 he lived in Pontoise and gathered around him Cézanne, Guillaumin, and Vignon, and it was he who brought Cézanne to Impressionism and helped him rid himself of his "somber manner." Thanks to Durand-Ruel, he began to become known. In 1874, he took part in the first Impressionist exhibition and insisted that Cézanne, whom he never ceased to encourage, should also be admitted. Talented young men were con-

tinually benefiting from his un-
ending kindness; he helped them
in their experiments and put up
with the enthusiasm of Gauguin,
Signac, Seurat, and Van Gogh.
At one time he even experiment-
ed with Pointillism, but he soon
discarded so rigid a system.
After 1884, he retired to Éragny,
near Gisors, where he painted
gardens and orchards in bloom,
and he paid visits to Rouen
(1896-1898), Dieppe, and Le
Havre. From 1893 until his
death he painted views of Paris
which, with their plunging vistas
of the boulevards and their range
of light effects, constituted a
series which even Monet might
have envied. "If one examines
Pissarro's art in its entirety,"
wrote Gauguin in 1902, "one
finds, despite its unevenness, not
only an intense instinct for art
which never contradicts itself, but
also an art which is essentially in-
tuitive in the best tradition. He
copied everyone, you say ? Why
not ? Everyone copied him, but
denied him. He was one of my
masters and I do not deny him."

Paysage à La Varenne-Saint-Hi-
laire, 1864.
Châtaigniers à Louveciennes,
1870.

La diligence à Louveciennes,
1870.
Entrée du village de Voisins,
1872.
La route de Louveciennes, 1872.
Le lavoir, Pontoise, 1872.
Pontoise, 1872.
Portrait de l'artiste, 1873.
La moisson à Montfoucault, 1876.
La diligence, route d'Ennery,
1877.
Chemin sous bois, en été, 1877.
Potager et arbres en fleurs, Pon-
toise, 1877.
Les toits rouges, 1877.
Chemin montant à travers
champs, 1879.
La brouette, *about* 1879/81.
Jeune fille à la baguette, 1881.
Effet de neige à Éragny, 1894.
L'église Saint-Jacques à Dieppe,
1901.

REDON Odilon. Born in Bordeaux, 1840; died in Paris, 1916.
Although he belonged to the
Impressionist generation, Odilon
Redon was, in fact, a man apart.
Too intelligent not to be independent, he found the Impressionist movement a little "dull-
witted." Bresdin, whom he had
known at Bordeaux and who
initiated him into the art of
engraving, had helped him to
discover the importance of the

extrasensory world: "True art lies in the apprehended reality." The imagination of the artist cannot create in a void, it depends essentially on the attentive observation of the real, even when it evokes a world of fantasy, indeed of the demoniac. "I have always felt the need to copy nature in the form of small, specific, accidental objects. It is only after expending every effort of will to achieve a minutely accurate representation of a blade of grass, a stone, a branch, or a section of an old wall, that I am driven as in torment to create something imaginary. External nature, thus apprehended and determined, becomes, in transformation, my source and my catalyst." Redon's uneventful life furnishes the biographer with but few interesting stories. It was Mallarmé's friendship which, after 1886, finally helped to achieve recognition of his work—an exact pictorial parallel of the experiments of the Symbolist poets. But it was not until after his death that Redon, who had already exercised an influence on the Nabis, was fully recognized. Later he was even hailed by the Surrealists as one of their earliest precursors.

Le Sacré-Cœur.
Portrait de Mme Odilon Redon, 1882.
Les yeux clos, 1890.
Vase de fleurs, le pavot rouge, *after* 1895.
Portrait de Gauguin, *about* 1903/05.
Bouquet de fleurs des champs, dans un vase à long col, *after* 1912.

RENOIR Pierre Auguste. Born in Limoges, 1841; died in Cagnes, 1919. Renoir was the son of a poor tailor. In 1845, the family went to live in Paris. He attended the elementary school, and at the age of thirteen he was apprenticed to a painter of chinaware. He decorated vases. His employer convinced his parents that he should be allowed to attend evening art classes and, whenever he had a spare moment, he went to the Louvre. He was determined to be a painter but, so as not to be a burden to his family, he saved up every penny in order to pay his own way. When he was twenty-one he entered the École des Beaux-Arts and the studio of Gleyre, where he made friends with Monet, Sisley, and Bazille. He accompanied them on their out-

RENOIR. HILLSIDE PATH IN TALL GRASS. *c.* 1877.

ings; together they went to Chailly in the forest of Fontainebleau, where, in 1864, he met Diaz. Despite the intervention of Corot and Daubigny, his work was rejected at the Salon of 1866. He fell under the influence of Courbet and Fantin; the portrait of *Lise* (1868) is the first work which affirms his own personality. Life was difficult, but his good humor sustained him. With Sisley, Bazille, and Monet he worked along the banks of the Seine at Bougival, where he painted *La Grenouillère* (1869). When war was declared he was conscripted, sent first to Bordeaux and then to Tarbes; but immediately upon the cessation of hostilities he returned to Paris, went back to work with Sisley in Bougival and Louveciennes, and often visited Monet at Argenteuil. Durand-Ruel, to whom he was introduced in 1873, bought his first pictures, which enabled him to set up in a large studio in Montmartre, at 35 Rue Saint-Georges.

As the Salon stubbornly remained closed to him, he joined his friends in the first of the group's exhibitions at Nadar's (1874). At the public auction in the Hôtel Drouot, which he had organized with Monet, Sisley, and Berthe Morisot, ten of his canvases failed to bring in even a hundred francs. The help of the collector

RENOIR. THE SWING. 1876.

RENOIR. MOULIN DE LA GALETTE. (DETAIL). 1876.

Chocquet and of the publisher Charpentier kept him going. A trip to Italy in 1881 acquainted him with the works of the Italian primitives and of Raphael, and he slowly began to break away from Impressionism. He admired Ingres and for some time adopted an extremely meticulous method of painting in which drawing played the dominant role. Nevertheless, after 1890, he returned to a less dry and more expansive style. As if obsessed by the female body, his principal subjects were usually nudes. He continued to make frequent trips both in France and abroad, but the precarious state of his health and the rheumatism with which he was afflicted forced him, after 1899, to retire to Cagnes in the Midi. In 1904, the retrospective exhibition of his work at the Salon d'Automne was an affirmation of his triumph. He continued to paint despite an attack of paralysis in 1912 which deprived him of the use of his limbs and obliged him to work in an armchair with his brush attached to his hand.

Renoir had renounced Impressionism because he considered himself primarily as the successor of those whom he had first admired—Boucher and Fragonard—the painters of the eighteenth century.

Portrait de William Sisley, 1864.
Portrait de Bazille, 1867.
Chalands sur la Seine, *about* 1869.
Portrait de Mme Théodore Charpentier, *about* 1869.
Femme demi-nue couchée : la rose, *about* 1872.
La Seine à Argenteuil, *about* 1873.

Portrait de Mme Hartmann, 1874.
Portrait de Monet, 1875.
Torse de femme au soleil, *about* 1875/76.
Chemin montant dans les hautes herbes, *about* 1876/78.
Jeune femme assise dans un jardin, *about* 1875/78.
La liseuse, *about* 1875/76.
Bords de Seine à Champrosay, 1876.
Portrait de Mme Alphonse Daudet, 1876.
Le Moulin de la Galette, 1876.
La balançoire, 1876.
Portrait de Mme Georges Charpentier, *about* 1877.

RENOIR. TORSO OF A WOMAN IN THE SUN. 1875-1876.

Jeune femme à la voilette, *about* 1875/77.

Portrait de modèle, *about* 1878/80.

A la Grenouillère, 1879.

Le pont du chemin de fer à Chatou, 1881.

Fête arabe à Alger, 1881.

Le ravin de la femme sauvage, *about* 1881.

Portrait de Théodore de Banville, *about* 1883.

Roses mousseuses, *about* 1890.

Roses dans un vase.

Jeunes filles au piano, 1892.

Portrait de fillette, *about* 1900/06.

Paysage : projet de tapisserie.

Portrait de Mme Gaston Bernheim de Villers, 1901.

Fillette au chapeau de paille, *about* 1908.

Ode aux fleurs, *about* 1903/09.

Jeune fille assise, 1909.

Nu couché, vu de dos, *about* 1909.

Portrait de Geneviève Bernheim de Villers, *about* 1910.

Portraits de M. et Mme Gaston Bernheim de Villers, 1910.

La toilette, femme se peignant, *about* 1910.

Gabrielle à la rose, 1911.

Jeune femme en bleu, 1913.

La liseuse blanche, *about* 1915/16.

Odalisque dormant, *about* 1915/17.

Les baigneuses, 1918.

ROUART Henri. Born in Paris, 1833; died there, 1912. Rouart occupied a position of more importance among the Impressionists than his work would lead one to suppose. His wealth and urbanity, his taste, both as a man and as a collector, allowed him, where his painter friends were concerned, to fill an unobtrusive but necessary role. He had known Degas at the lycée; he renewed their friendship in 1870 and when the aging artist became almost blind and increasingly misanthropic, he found a warm welcome in Rouart's house in the Rue de Lisbonne. Paul Valéry, who in his youth was a frequent visitor to the house, wrote: "He loved only those true values which he could appreciate in more than one field. The same man who appreciated and, very early, acquired works by Millet, Corot, Daumier, Manet—and El Greco—owed his fortune to his mechanical constructions, to his inventions which he carried from the realms of pure theory to that of technique, and from technique to industrial practicability . . .'' From the beginning, Henri Rouart shared in all the vicissitudes of the Impressionist group and, since he

ROUSSEAU. THE SNAKE CHARMER. 1907.

exhibited with them seven times, was one of their most faithful associates. But because he allowed himself to become thoroughly absorbed by business he was unable to devote the necessary time to painting, and today he is considered a minor painter.

La terrasse, *about* 1880.
L'église Saint-Michel à Murano.

ROUSSEAU Henri Julien, known as Douanier. Born at Laval in 1844, died at Paris in 1910. He was the son of a tin vendor, became a saxophonist in the Infantry, and in 1869 settled in Paris where he worked as a customs official. He claimed to have taken part in the French expedition to Mexico, which was almost certainly a myth, but nevertheless one which had a singular hold on his imagination. He was nearly forty years old when he began to paint, and he left the customs service in 1893, continuing to practice various trades (copyist, shop-keeper, teacher of drawing and music). From 1886 onwards, he exhibited at the Salon des Indépendants, and from 1905 onwards at the Salon d'Automne. Pissarro, Gauguin, Seurat, Jarry and Gourmont all became interested in his work, he met Apollinaire in 1906 and Wilhem Uhde in 1907; when he began to be famous, the famous banquet in his honor was held at Picasso's studio in the Bateau-Lavoir. His pictures were bought by Uhde, Vollard, Soffici, Serge Férat, and Delaunay. His last months were saddened by an unhappy love affair and he died in the Hôpital Necker in 1910.

Rousseau is considered to be the greatest master of naïve painting, for his art combines a spontaneous vision of reality with an imaginary universe of great plastic and poetical power, in which he allied audacity with innocence, monumental composition with minute detail. His many famous pictures include portraits of himself or of friends (*Loti,* 1891; *Apollinaire,* 1909), scenes of popular life (*A Wedding in the Country,* 1905; *The Cart of Père Juniet,* 1908), bouquets of flowers, views of Paris and its suburbs (*In the Parc Montsouris,* 1895), allegories (*War,* 1894; *The Dream,* 1910), and exotic scenes inspired by his mythical Mexico (*The Sleeping Gipsy,* 1897; *The Snake Charmer,* 1907). P. G.

La guerre ou la Chevauchée de la Discorde, 1894.
La charmeuse de serpents, 1907.

SEURAT Georges. Born in Paris, 1859; died there, 1891. Son of a court attendant, he first attended a municipal art school, then, for two years, the École des Beaux-Arts (1878-1880). Seeking to discover the secret of Veronese, Ingres, and Delacroix, he believed that he would find it in Chevreul's study of "the simultaneous contrast of colors." Between 1881 and 1883, he devoted himself primarily to drawings. His first large canvas, *Une Baignade,* was rejected by the jury of the 1884 Salon, and so he helped to precipitate the formation and was one of the founding members of the Société des

SEURAT.
LE CIRQUE.
1891.

Artistes Indépendants, presided over by Odilon Redon. He allied himself with Signac and, together, they created the technique of Neo-Impressionism. For them it was a question of rejecting Monet's empiricism and of constructing something rational and scientific, of finding an infallible recipe for every master-piece. With the systematic approach which is typical of him, Seurat worked very slowly; it took him two years to paint *Un Dimanche d'Été à la Grande Jatte* (1884-1886) which required at least thirty-eight studies in oil and twenty-three preparatory drawings. His principal works were *La Parade* (1887-1888), *Les*

Poseuses (1887-1888), *Le Chahut* (1889-1890); his sudden death on March 29, 1891, at the age of thirty-two, prevented him from completing his final work, *Le Cirque*. "At the time of Seurat's death," said Signac, "the critics acknowledged his talent, but maintained that he had left not a single work. It seems to me, on the contrary, that he gave, and gave superbly, all that he had to give. He had surveyed everything and had established, almost definitively, the use of black and white, harmony of line, composition, and the contrast and harmony of color. What more can one ask of a painter?"

Esquisse pour "Un dimanche dans l'Ile de la Grande Jatte", 1884-1886.
Poseuse de face, 1887.
Poseuse de dos, 1887.
Poseuse de profil, 1887.
Port-en-Bessin, avant-port, marée haute, 1888.
Esquisse du Cirque, 1891.
Le Cirque, 1891.

SISLEY Alfred. Born in Paris, 1839; died in Moret-sur-Loing, 1899. Born of British parents, Sisley spent all his life in France, apart from a few infrequent visits to London. After a half-hearted venture into commerce he joined Gleyre's studio (1862). His essentially poetic feeling for nature, both dream-like and delicate, evoked memories of Daubigny, Lépine, and Corot. In London, in 1871, he met Durand-Ruel who sponsored an important exhibition of his works in 1883. Financially ruined by the death of his father, he still went on painting. Marly, Bougival, Louveciennes (1872-1876), Sèvres, Suresnes, Saint-Mammès (1877-1882), and Moret, where he finally settled, are the motifs which he repeated tirelessly with the same feeling of melancholy. From 1885, more and more influenced by Monet, he adopted the Impressionist technique and colors. Leading an extremely withdrawn existence, he became touchy and irritable and allowed himself to remain practically unknown among his generation. "He watched all the joys of life depart from him one by one, except the joy of painting, which remained always."

Vue du canal Saint-Martin, 1870.
Le canal, 1872.

SISLEY. BOAT DURING A FLOOD. 1876.

Le repos au bord du ruisseau, 1872.

La passerelle d'Argenteuil, 1872.

La place d'Argenteuil, 1872.

Bateaux à l'écluse de Bougival, 1873.

La route, vue du chemin de Sèvres, 1873.

Route de Louveciennes, *about* 1873.

L'Ile Saint-Denis, *about* 1872.

Le village de Voisins, 1874.

Les régates, *about* 1874.

La forge à Marly-le-Roi, 1875.

La neige à Marly-le-Roi, 1875.

La barque pendant l'inondation, 1876.

L'inondation à Port-Marly, 1876.

La Seine à Suresnes, 1877.

La neige à Louveciennes, 1878.

Lisière de forêt au printemps, 1880.

Temps de neige à Veneux-Nadon, *about* 1879/82.

La route à l'orée du bois, *about* 1883.

Saint-Mammès, 1885.

Cour de ferme, 1884 *or* 1888.

La Seine vue des coteaux de By, *about* 1885/89.

Trembles et acacias, 1889.

Moret, les bords du Loing, 1892.

Le canal du Loing, 1892.

T O U L O U S E - L A U T R E C
Henri. Born in Albi, 1864; died in Malromé, 1901. Born into the old French aristocracy he was brought up in the Château de Malromé by a pious mother and a father devoted to falconry, horses, and hunting. He was educated in Paris at the Lycée Condorcet, but his already delicate health was further undermined by two successive falls which left him an invalid. Even

SISLEY.
SNOW AT
LOUVECIENNES.
1878.

when he was a small child he used to draw and, on the advice of Princeteau, a friend of his father and a painter of animals, he devoted himself to painting. In 1882, he went to Bonnat's studio in the École des Beaux-Arts where his master found his drawing "atrocious"; then he went to the studio of Cormon.

At that time he made the acquaintance of Émile Bernard, Anquetin, and Van Gogh, who impressed him greatly. His friends helped him discover bohemian Paris. In 1884, he set himself up in the Rue Tourlaque in Montmartre, not far from the studio of Degas. Thenceforth, the "Mirliton" and the "Moulin Rouge" were like

TOULOUSE-LAUTREC.
WOMAN
WITH GLOVES.
c. 1889-1890.

home to him. Valentin le Désossé, Jane Avril, Grille d'Égout,
La Goulue, Casque d'Or became his friends. He illustrated
Bruant's songs, drew posters,
and decorated La Goulue's booth
at the Foire du Trône (1895).
The sentimentality of the under-
world left him untouched. An
aristocrat through and through,
he was drawn to people who were
out of the ordinary regardless of
their origins, and he applied
himself to defining them without
any of the cruelty of Degas, yet
at the same time without moraliz-
ing. Passionately interested in
horses, both because of his background and because they were
incarnations of the very essence
of beauty—nobility, elegance,
power, and speed—he could

73

be found in the paddock at Longchamp by day and in the bar of the "Moulin Rouge" at night. But the alcohol which ate into his system and his disordered life left him a prey to the most terrifying obsessions. He was sent to a mental hospital in Neuilly (1899) to take a cure for alcoholism. It was during his stay in the clinic that he executed —from memory—the famous series of drawings of the circus. Struck down by an attack of paralysis at the age of thirty-seven, he died in his mother's arms in the Château de Malromé on September 9, 1901.

Portrait de Justine Dieuhl, *about* 1889/90.

La femme aux gants, *about* 1889/90.

La femme au boa noir, *about* 1892.

TOULOUSE–LAUTREC.
SEATED GIRL,
BACK VIEW.
1896.

VAN GOGH. THE RESTAURANT DE LA SIRÈNE. *c.* 1887-1888.

Femme tirant son bas, *about* 1894.
Femme devant un lit, *about* 1894/95.
La clownesse Cha-U-Kao, 1895.
Panneaux pour la baraque de la Goulue :
1. La danse de la Goulue et de Valentin le Désossé.
2. La danse de la Goulue, ou les Almées, 1895.
La toilette, 1896.

Portrait de Paul Leclercq, 1897.
Portrait de Louis Bouglé, 1898.

VAN GOGH Vincent. Born at Groot-Zundert (Holland) in 1853, died at Auvers-sur-Oise in 1890. Van Gogh's tragic life may be said to be a dialogue between the man and his image. Many generations of his family had been Protestant pastors but also pict-

VAN GOGH. THE CHURCH AT AUVERS. 1890.

ure dealers, and Van Gogh was long torn between the two vocations, uncertain whether to serve the humble of this earth or to devote himself to art, but in the end he was to choose painting

VAN GOGH.
SELF-PORTRAIT.
1890.

as the means of attaining his mystic ideal. In 1869 he went to work with the dealer Goupil who had taken over his uncle Vincent's gallery at The Hague. He spent various periods in the Paris and London branches and suddenly discovered Japanese art which came as a revelation to him. After experiencing a mystical crisis, he went to the Borinage region of Belgium as a lay-preacher ("I wish to console the humble") but his attempt ended in utter failure and he went back to his parents' home at Etten. After an unhappy liaison with a prostitute, he found refuge and consolation in painting, expressing his love of poor, humble people in such pictures as *The Weavers, The Potato Eaters* (1885) and *Boots*. In November 1885, his brother Theo who had been looking after him since their father's death, sent him some money. After discovering Rubens at Antwerp, Vincent suddenly decided to join his brother in Paris

(March 1886). There, he was enraptured by the art of Delacroix, Sisley, Gauguin, Monticelli, and Seurat and by their use of light and color. This marked the end of his first artistic period, influenced by the lessons he had been given by his cousin, the painter Mauve, at The Hague, and he began to make the whole Impressionist experiment again on his own. But such an art, essentially dependent on the play of light an color, was not enough for him and his driving inner urge sent him southwards in search of those clear-cut, basic patterns and colors which had so attracted him and caught his attention in Japanese art.

In February 1888 be arrived at Arles ("It's the Orient !") and rejecting the lessons of the Impressionists, painted more than two hundred pictures in an joyful explosion of creation *(The Langlois Bridge at Arles, The Mousmé, Boats at the Saintes-Maries, The Postman Roulin, Sunflowers, Vincent's Bedroom).* But he was mentally unbalanced, and soon began to suffer from hallucinations, being obsessed by the idea of death, and to save himself from entirely succumbing he worked with all the energy of despair. His mental crises became more frequent, and he called Gauguin to join him but the help he hoped for from his friend was not forthcoming, for they quarreled bitterly, and their liaison ended with the terrible scene on Christmas eve, when Van Gogh sliced his own ear off with a razor. Interned at the asylum of Saint-Rémy (1889), Van Gogh worked for a year, in between two fits of madness, like a man possessed, painting flame-like, delirious landscapes with huge whirling suns as though the whole of nature had been possessed by some mad frenzy. After Theo had interceded on his behalf, he was moved to the house of Dr. Gachet in Auvers-sur-Oise for observation (May 1890). There, he found some peace, affection and care, but he was afraid of lapsing back into insanity and—afraid of himself. On July 29th, 1890, he committed suicide, to escape from that "extreme solitude" he feared so much and had expressed, just before his death, in his painting *Cornfield with Crows.*

Tête de paysanne, 1885.

VAN GOGH. PORTRAIT OF DR. GACHET. 1890.

Fritillaires couronne impériale dans un vase de cuivre, 1886.

La guinguette, *about* 1886.

Le restaurant de la Sirène, *about* 1887/88.

Campement de bohémiens, les roulottes, 1888.

Portrait du peintre Boch, 1888.

La chambre de Van Gogh à Arles, 1889.

Le jardin du Dr Gachet, 1890.

Mlle Gachet au jardin, 1890.

L'église d'Auvers, 1890.

Roses et anémones, 1890.

Deux fillettes, 1890.

Chaumes à Cordeville, 1890.

Portrait du Dr Gachet, 1890.

Portrait de l'artiste par lui-même, 1890.

ACHEVÉ D'IMPRIMER
EN MAI 1972 PAR JEAN MUSSOT